The Ohio State Buckeyes

BY
MARK STEWART

NORWOOD HOUSE 🏠 PRESS

CHICAGO, ILLINOIS

Norwood House Press
P.O. Box 316598
Chicago, Illinois 60631

For information regarding Norwood House Press, please visit our website at:
www.norwoodhousepress.com or call 866-565-2900.

All photos courtesy of The Associated Press except the following:
Fiction House, Inc. (14); Street & Smith Publications, Inc. (20);
Author's Collection (28, 35, 37 bottom left, 40 bottom both); Topps, Inc. (36);
Bowman Gum Co. (39); OSU Police Dept. (32, 40 top left, 41 both);
Press Pass/RC2 South, Inc. (40 bottom left); Matt Richman (48).
Cover Photo: David Maxwell/Getty Images.

Special thanks to Topps, Inc.

Editor: Mike Kennedy
Designer: Ron Jaffe
Project Management: Black Book Partners, LLC.
Research: Joshua Zaffos

Library of Congress Cataloging-in-Publication Data

Stewart, Mark, 1960-
    The Ohio State Buckeyes / by Mark Stewart.
      p. cm. -- (Team spirit : college football)
    Includes bibliographical references and index.
    Summary: "Presents the history, accomplishments and key personalities of
the Ohio State University football team. Includes timelines, quotes, maps,
glossary and website"--Provided by publisher.
    ISBN-13: 978-1-59953-277-6 (library edition : alk. paper)
    ISBN-10: 1-59953-277-8 (library edition : alk. paper) 1. Ohio State
Buckeyes (Football team)--Juvenile literature. 2. Ohio State
University--Football--Juvenile literature. I. Title.
    GV958.O35S745 2009
    796.332'630977157--dc22
                                                    2008026007

COVER PHOTO: The Buckeyes congratulate each other during the 2003 season.

Table of Contents

SPORTS WORDS & VOCABULARY WORDS: In this book, you will find many words that are new to you. You may also see familiar words used in new ways. The glossary on page 46 gives the meanings of football words, as well as "everyday" words that have special football meanings. These words appear in **bold type** throughout the book. The glossary on page 47 gives the meanings of vocabulary words that are not related to football. They appear in ***bold italic type*** throughout the book.

Meet the Buckeyes

Football can be a complicated game. The Ohio State University Buckeyes make it look simple. Hit hard, think fast, and never give up—in most games, these are the things that help a team win. That is how the Buckeyes play football. It is why they have become one of college football's greatest teams.

The Ohio State *campus* is located in Columbus, which also happens to be the state capital. During the early 1900s, football "grew up" in this part of the country. The sport has a long and proud *tradition* there.

This book tells the story of the Buckeyes football team. They are part of the **Big Ten Conference**, a group of schools that take their football very seriously. No one, however, takes football more seriously than the Ohio State players—except for the Ohio State fans. When they get together to root for their Buckeyes, their hopes and dreams hang on every play.

The Buckeyes celebrate a big defensive play during their 2002 championship season.

Way Back When

Back in the 1880s, football was wildly popular among schools in the East. The sport, however, had yet to catch on in other parts of the country. That soon began to change. By 1890, "football fever" had reached the Midwest, including the Ohio State campus. A group of students led by George Cole arranged a game with Ohio Wesleyan University that spring. The Buckeyes won the contest, and the school's football tradition was born.

In 1913, Ohio State joined the Western Conference, which later became the Big Ten Conference. The school's first great player, Charles "Chic" Harley, led the Buckeyes to conference championships in 1916 and 1917.

Beginning in 1920, the champion of the Big Ten played the champion of the Pac-10 (the major conference on the West Coast) in the **Rose Bowl**. Many fans viewed the contest as the most exciting game of the season. Ohio State went to the Rose Bowl for the first time in 1950 and returned 12 more times over the next five *decades*. The Buckeyes won the game six times.

After four of those victories, the Buckeyes were crowned national champions.

Their most famous coaches were Paul Brown and Woody Hayes. Brown looked for quick players who could **outsmart** their opponents. He would go on to a legendary coaching career with the Cleveland Browns. Hayes built a powerful running attack that slowly wore down the opposing defense. His strategy was known as, "Three yards and a cloud of dust."

The Buckeyes had many **All-Americans** over the years. During the 1920s and 1930s, their stars included Wes Fesler, Gus Zarnas, and Gomer Jones. During the 1940s and 1950s, Les Horvath, Bill Willis, Aurelius Thomas, Vic Janowicz, Jim Parker, Warren Amling, and Howard "Hopalong" Cassady were among the best players in the nation. The Buckeyes raised national championship banners four times from 1942 to 1961.

Over the next few years, however, the team often struggled to win. In 1968, Hayes broke his own rule and put a group of teenagers into the starting **lineup**. They became known as the "Super Sophomores" and led Ohio State back to the national title. Mike Sensibaugh,

LEFT: Paul Brown, the coach who led Ohio State to its first national championship, in 1942. **ABOVE**: Woody Hayes, the greatest coach in school history.

Jack Tatum, Rex Kern, Jim Otis, and Jim Stillwagon were the heart of that amazing team. Several players from the 1968 club were seniors in 1970, when the Buckeyes won a share of the national championship.

After that national championship, the Buckeyes went more than 30 years without finishing the season as the nation's best team. Still, Ohio State had some of the top players in college football, including Archie Griffin, Pete Johnson, Neal Colzie, John Hicks, Tom Cousineau, John Frank, Chris Spielman, Marcus Marek, and Cris Carter. Griffin ran for more than 100 yards in 31 games in a row and became the first player to win the **Heisman Trophy** twice.

The Buckeyes continued to put great players on the field in the 1990s. Their offensive stars included running back Eddie George, receivers Terry Glenn and David Boston, and linemen Orlando Pace and Korey Stringer. Their top defensive players were Steve Tovar, Antoine Winfield, Dan Wilkinson, Mike Vrabel, and Andy Katzenmoyer. In 2001, Jim Tressel was hired to coach the team. His job was to rebuild the Buckeyes and lead them back to the top of college football.

LEFT: Archie Griffin sprints to daylight against Indiana University.
ABOVE: Eddie George, one of Ohio State's best players during the 1990s.

21st Century

In 2002, Jim Tressel guided Ohio State to its first championship since the 1970 season. The Buckeyes did not lose a single game that year. They won with the kind of old-fashioned football that brought young fans out of their seats and made **old-timers** smile.

Good defense and a rugged running game helped Ohio State win many close games, including the championship contest against the University of Miami. The Buckeyes continued their success in the years that followed. They shared the Big Ten championship in 2005, and won it again in 2006 and 2007. The team fell one victory short of another national title in both 2006 and 2007.

As in past decades, Ohio State continues to send many great players into **professional** football. Almost every pro team has at least one Buckeye on its **roster**. Stars such as Will Allen, Troy Smith, Nate Clements, Anthony Gonzalez, and A.J. Hawk now play in the colors of their professional teams. In their hearts, however, they will always wear Buckeye scarlet and gray, and hear echoes of the 100,000 fans that cheered them on in Ohio Stadium.

Anthony Gonzalez and Ted Ginn Jr. jump for joy after a touchdown during the 2006 season. Both players went on to the pros.

Home Turf

In the early years of Ohio State football, the Buckeyes played at tiny Ohio Field. In 1922, they moved into Ohio Stadium. It eventually became known as the "Horseshoe" for its U-like shape. Others called it the "House That Harley Built" in honor of Ohio State's first great star, Charles "Chic" Harley.

For 20 seasons beginning in 1970, Ohio State played on **artificial** turf. The team switched back to grass in 1990. The Buckeyes installed a new artificial playing surface in 2007.

Today, Ohio Stadium holds more than 100,000 people. Outside the stadium is Buckeye Grove. There, the school plants a tree for each of Ohio State's All-Americans.

BY THE NUMBERS

- *Ohio Stadium has 102,329 seats.*
- *The first night game at Ohio Stadium was played on September 14th, 1985.*
- *The original cost of Ohio Stadium was $1.3 million. The school renovated the stadium before the 2001 season at a cost of $194 million.*

Ohio Stadium is always packed with excited fans on game day. Here, they are signaling the "O" for "O-H-I-O."

Dressed for Success

The Buckeyes got their name from a type of oak tree that grows in Ohio. It drops an acorn that looks like the eye of a male deer, or buck. Ohio State players have been called "Buckeyes" for many decades. The name became official in 1950.

The school colors are a deep red—known as scarlet—and gray. The students chose these colors in 1878. Orange and black were also considered, but Princeton University was already using them.

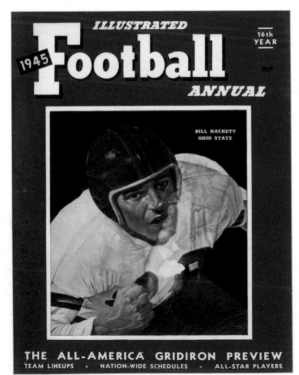

The team's helmets are silver with scarlet, black, and white striping. The helmets of many players are covered with small stickers that feature the leaf from a buckeye. Ohio State's coaches award these stickers to players who have made great plays in a game. Woody Hayes started the tradition in 1968.

Bill Hackett models the Ohio State uniform from the 1940s.

UNIFORM BASICS

The football uniform has three important parts—

- Helmet
- Jersey
- Pants

Helmets used to be made out of leather, and they did not have facemasks—ouch! Today, helmets are made of super-strong plastic. The uniform top, or jersey, is made of thick fabric. It fits snugly around a player so that tacklers cannot grab it and pull him down. The pants come down just over the knees.

There is a lot more to a football uniform than what you see on the outside. Air can be pumped inside the helmet to give it a snug, padded fit. The jersey covers shoulder pads, and sometimes a rib protector called a flak jacket. The pants include pads that protect the hips, thighs, *tailbone*, and knees.

Football teams have two sets of uniforms—one dark and one light. This makes it easier to tell two teams apart on the field. Almost all teams wear their dark uniforms at home and their light ones on the road.

Troy Smith wears Ohio State's home uniform during a 2006 game. His helmet is covered with Buckeye stickers.

We're Number 1!

Ohio State's first national championship came in 1942. At the beginning of the year, no one knew how the Buckeyes—or any other college team—would do. More than half of America's players had **enlisted** to fight in World War II. Coach Paul Brown relied heavily on **tailback** Les Horvath, who was one of only three seniors on the team. Bill Willis, the school's first African-American star, led the defense.

The Buckeyes lost only one game in 1942. That was especially impressive because Ohio State played twice against military teams made up of college and professional players. The Buckeyes won both games. The team also recorded a 21–7 victory over the University of Michigan in a heavy rainstorm. Near the end of the season, the two teams ahead of Ohio State in the rankings—Boston College and Georgia Tech—lost badly. The Buckeyes were named champions of college football.

Ohio State returned to the top of college football in 1954. Coach Woody Hayes led one of the most exciting teams in the

nation. His best player was a great runner and star defender named Howard "Hopalong" Cassady. In a showdown with the powerful University of Wisconsin, Cassady **intercepted** a pass and ran 88 yards for a touchdown. Against Michigan, the Buckeyes made an amazing **goal-line stand**. They finished the year with a 20–7 victory in the Rose Bowl and shared the national title with UCLA.

During the 1950s, Ohio State helped make the Big Ten the most powerful conference in college football. In 1957, four Big Ten teams began the year ranked in the Top 10. The Buckeyes were not one of them, however. After Ohio State lost its opening game, no one gave the team much of a chance. But Hayes convinced his players that they

LEFT: Les Horvath, one of the stars for the 1942 Buckeyes.
ABOVE: Howard "Hopalong" Cassady breaks free in a 1955 game against the University of Illinois.

could do anything, and Ohio State did not lose again that year. The team's toughest game came against the University of Iowa. The Buckeyes scored the winning touchdown late in the game behind the strong running of a young fullback named Bob White. Ohio State shared the championship again, this time with Auburn University.

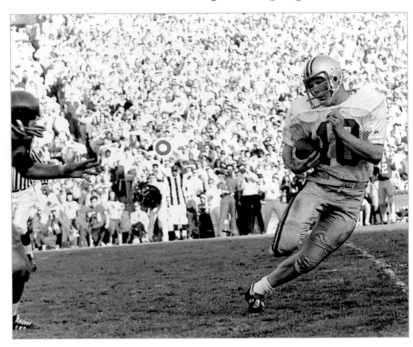

In 1968, the Buckeyes won the national title, thanks to a group of sophomores who showed great skill and team spirit in practice. Though Hayes preferred to play juniors and seniors, he knew his young stars were too talented to sit on the bench. Hayes started 10 sophomores that season, including quarterback Rex Kern, running back John Brockington, and defensive backs Jack Tatum and Mike Sensibaugh. The Buckeyes were *sensational*—they did not lose a single game. On the way to their fifth national championship, they beat four of the country's best teams. Their two most impressive victories were a 50–14 blowout of Michigan and a 27–16 *rout* of USC in the Rose Bowl. In 1970, Brockington, Kern,

and the other sophomores were seniors. They led the Buckeyes to a 9–1 season and a share of the national championship.

In 2002, coach Jim Tressel led the school to its first national title in 32 years. The star of that team was Maurice Clarett, a freshman runner with great size and speed. He helped Ohio State control the ball and wear down opposing defenses. At the end of most games, the Buckeyes felt strong and energized, while their opponents were weak and tired.

After exciting wins over Purdue University and Michigan, the Buckeyes played the University of Miami for the national championship. It was one of the most thrilling games in history. It took two **overtime** periods before Ohio State beat the Hurricanes and celebrated the seventh title in school history.

LEFT: Rex Kern avoids a tackle during the Rose Bowl in 1969.
ABOVE: Coach Jim Tressel and his players celebrate their win over the Miami Hurricanes.

Go-To Guys

These great Buckeyes have won major awards.

LES HORVATH
Running Back/Quarterback

• BORN: 10/12/1921 • DIED: 11/14/1995 • PLAYED FOR VARSITY: 1940–1942 & 1944

Les Horvath played three years for the Buckeyes and then enrolled in dental school. When Ohio State ran short of players during World War II, he returned to the team. Horvath led the Buckeyes to the 1942 national championship and won the 1944 Heisman Trophy.

VIC JANOWICZ
Running Back

• BORN: 2/26/1930 • DIED: 2/27/1996 • PLAYED FOR VARSITY: 1949-1951

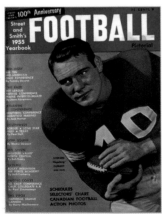

Vic Janowicz was a great runner, passer, kicker, **blocker**, and defensive player. He won the Heisman Trophy in 1950 and was also the star of Ohio State's baseball team. After graduation, he played football for the Washington Redskins and baseball for the Pittsburgh Pirates.

HOWARD CASSADY
Running Back

• BORN: 3/2/1934 • PLAYED FOR VARSITY: 1952–1955

Howard "Hopalong" Cassady got his nickname from a popular movie hero. Cassady was a hero to Ohio State fans for his running and defense. In 1955, he won the Heisman Trophy and was named America's Athlete of the Year.

ARCHIE GRIFFIN   Running Back

• BORN: 8/21/1954   • PLAYED FOR VARSITY: 1972–1975

When Archie Griffin joined the Buckeyes, many fans felt he was too small to run the ball for Ohio State. All he did was lead the team in rushing yards four times and win three Big Ten rushing championships. Griffin was the only player ever to win the Heisman Trophy twice and start in four Rose Bowls.

EDDIE GEORGE   Running Back

• BORN: 9/24/1973   • PLAYED FOR VARSITY: 1992–1995

Eddie George sat on the bench for two seasons because he **fumbled** too often. Once he learned to hold onto the football, he became the team's best player as a junior and senior. In 1995, George set an Ohio State record when he ran for 1,927 yards. He also won the Heisman Trophy that year.

TROY SMITH   Quarterback

• BORN: 7/20/1984

• PLAYED FOR VARSITY: 2003–2006

An injury to Ohio State's starting quarterback gave Troy Smith a chance to play during his sophomore season. Smith became a star when he led the Buckeyes to victory over Michigan. He was as dangerous running with the ball as he was passing it. Smith was named **Most Valuable Player (MVP)** of the **Fiesta Bowl** as a junior and won the Heisman Trophy his senior year.

LEFT: "Hopalong" Cassady   **ABOVE**: Troy Smith

CHIC HARLEY   Running Back

- BORN: 9/15/1895 • DIED: 4/21/1974
- PLAYED FOR VARSITY: 1916–1917 & 1919

Chic Harley was an outstanding runner and kicker who led Ohio State to its first victory ever over Michigan. He left school in 1918 to become

a fighter pilot during World War I, and then returned for one more amazing season. Harley got Buckeye fans so excited about football that the school built Ohio Stadium in the 1920s.

WES FESLER   End

- BORN: 6/29/1908 • DIED: 7/30/1989
- PLAYED FOR VARSITY: 1929–1930

Wes Fesler was a one-man wrecking crew for the Buckeyes. On offense, he was a powerful blocker and sure-handed receiver. On defense, he was a hard tackler. Fesler was also one of the finest kickers in the game. Not only was Fesler an All-American in football, he was the star of the school's basketball and baseball teams, too.

JIM PARKER   Lineman

- BORN: 4/3/1934 • DIED: 7/18/2005 • PLAYED FOR VARSITY: 1954–1956

Jim Parker was a fierce blocker who opened holes in the line for Ohio State's running backs. He was a major reason the Buckeyes won the national championship in 1954. Parker was a big man who was very quick for his size. That helped him become a star on defense, too.

PAUL WARFIELD Running Back/Receiver

• BORN: 11/28/1942 • PLAYED FOR VARSITY: 1961–1963

Paul Warfield was a sprinter and hurdler for the Ohio State track team. His blazing speed and quick moves also made him a star for the football team. Warfield started his career with the Buckeyes as a running back and later became one of the team's best receivers.

CRIS CARTER Receiver

• BORN: 11/25/1965 • PLAYED FOR VARSITY: 1984–1986

Cris Carter went to Ohio State to please his mother, who was a big fan of the Buckeyes. He became the school's first receiver to be named an All-American. Carter had great speed and body control, and he caught almost every ball he got his hands on.

ORLANDO PACE Offensive Lineman

• BORN: 11/4/1975 • PLAYED FOR VARSITY: 1993–1996

Ohio State has had many great linemen, but Orlando Pace might have been the best. He stood 6′ 7″ and weighed 325 pounds, but moved with the quickness of a running back. Pace specialized in the "pancake block"—when he smashed into a defender, that player often ended up flat on his back.

LEFT: Chic Harley   **ABOVE**: Paul Warfield

BILL WILLIS   Lineman

- BORN: 10/5/1921   • DIED: 11/27/2007   • PLAYED FOR VARSITY: 1941–1944

Bill Willis weighed just 200 pounds when coach Paul Brown asked him to try out for the defensive line. Brown believed that Willis's speed and

strength would give him an edge over bigger, slower players. Brown was right—Willis became a great tackler who led the Buckeyes to the national championship in 1942.

JIM HOUSTON   End

- BORN: 11/3/1937

- PLAYED FOR VARSITY: 1957–1959

Jim Houston played end on offense and defense. When the Buckeyes had the ball, he was a good blocker and receiver. On defense, he moved quickly and hit hard. Houston was an All-American twice for Ohio State.

JIM STILLWAGON   Defensive Lineman

- BORN: 2/11/1949   • PLAYED FOR VARSITY: 1967–1970

Jim Stillwagon was one of the "super sophomores" who led Ohio State to an **undefeated** season and national championship in 1968. Stillwagon was named All-American twice. He was also the first winner of the Lombardi Award, which honors the best lineman or linebacker in college football.

TOM COUSINEAU   **Linebacker**

- BORN: 5/6/1957
- PLAYED FOR VARSITY: 1982–1985

Tom Cousineau seemed to be everywhere at once. During his career as a Buckeye, he set school records with 29 tackles in a game and 211 in a season. He was named MVP of two bowl games and was a two-time All-American.

CHRIS SPIELMAN   **Linebacker**

- BORN: 10/11/1965
- PLAYED FOR VARSITY: 1984–1987

Chris Spielman was big, smart, fast, and ***enthusiastic***. When the Buckeyes needed to stop an opponent, they looked to him for leadership. Spielman was one of the best players in the nation in 1987. He was voted Ohio State's MVP and won the Lombardi Award that year.

A.J. HAWK   **Linebacker**

- BORN: 1/6/1984   • PLAYED FOR VARSITY: 2002–2005

A.J. Hawk was the best linebacker in the nation in 2004 and 2005. He always seemed to know what the offense would do, whether it was a run or pass. Hawk won the Lombardi Award as a senior.

LEFT: Bill Willis   **ABOVE**: Chris Spielman

On the Sidelines

Ask football fans about Ohio State football coaches, and Woody Hayes is the first name that comes to mind. Hayes was on the sidelines for the Buckeyes from 1951 to 1978. During that time, he recorded 205 wins, 13 Big Ten championships, and five national championships. He was famous for his hot temper. Hayes would not accept anything but the best from his players. When he got less than their best, he could explode. The Buckeyes were a powerful running team when Hayes coached them.

Two other coaches led the Buckeyes to national championships. The first was Paul Brown. He liked quick-thinking, fast-moving players. Brown was one of the smartest coaches in history. Later he became a great coach in the **National Football League (NFL)**.

The other coach who guided the Buckeyes to the national title was Jim Tressel. In 2002—just his second year as coach—he led Ohio State to the first 14–0 season in college football history. Like Hayes, Tressel became a very popular coach. Unlike Hayes, he had a calm, cool style.

Woody Hayes watches the action from the sideline. The Buckeyes won the national title four times with him as their coach.

Rivals

Since the 1940s, the final game of the year for Ohio State has been its meeting with the Wolverines of Michigan. In most seasons, the winner of this game is crowned conference champion. Sometimes, that team also goes on to win the national championship. Ohio State and Michigan may be college football's greatest rivals.

The two schools first met on the football field in 1897. The Buckeyes, however, did not beat Michigan for the first time until 1919. Ohio State began to even things up in 1934. They won four times in a row against Michigan and did not allow the Wolverines to score a single point.

Things really heated up in the 1940s when both schools were ranked among the best teams in the nation. Michigan got the better of Ohio State during these years. The Buckeyes soon got their revenge. From 1951 to 1968, they won 12 of the 18 games

played between the schools. Woody Hayes coached Ohio State during this period. He hated to lose to Michigan.

Over the next few decades, the rivalry see-sawed back and forth. But when Jim Tressel took over as coach for Ohio State, the Buckeyes gained a big edge. In 2002, they won 14–9 with an exciting late-game touchdown. In 2006, Ohio State and Michigan met for the first time with the teams ranked first and second in the country. The Buckeyes won 42–39 in what many called the "Game of the *Century*."

LEFT: Pins such as this one have been around since the 1920s.
ABOVE: Michigan tacklers have no chance of catching speedy Antonio Pittman. He scored a long touchdown for the Buckeyes in the 2006 game.

One Great Day

T he 2002 Buckeyes finished their regular season at 13–0. In six of those victories, the game was close until the clock ran out. So when Ohio State prepared to face the Miami Hurricanes in the Fiesta Bowl for the national championship, most fans were expecting a tight game. They never imagined just how tight it would be.

The Buckeyes were a mix of old and new. Their star player on defense was Mike Doss. He was already good enough to play safety in the NFL, but he decided to stay in Columbus for his senior year. Will Allen, another talented defensive back, would join Doss in the pros in a few months. The team's quarterback, Craig Krenzel, was in his first season as a starter. Their powerful running back, Maurice Clarett, had been playing high school football a year earlier.

History did not favor the Buckeyes against Miami. No college team had ever had a perfect 14-win season. After one quarter, Miami led

7–0. In the second quarter, Krenzel and Clarett each scored a touchdown to give the Buckeyes a 14–7 lead. With time running out in the fourth quarter, Ohio State was still ahead, but now only 17–14. When Miami kicked a field goal, the game went into overtime.

The Hurricanes scored a touchdown to begin the extra period. Ohio State needed a touchdown to tie the game. On fourth down, Krenzel threw incomplete to Chris Gamble in the end zone, but the referee called a penalty on Miami. With new life, Krenzel scored on a short run to tie the game and force a second overtime.

In the next period, Ohio State got the ball first. Clarett scored on a five-yard run to put the Buckeyes in front. Miami then drove to the 1 yard line. That's when the Buckeyes stiffened. Thanks to an amazing goal-line stand, Ohio State won 31–24 and celebrated its first championship in 34 years.

It Really Happened

Can a player run so fast that he flies right out of his shoes? Most of the fans in Ohio Stadium for the 1984 game against Illinois would have said no—if they had not seen it happen with their own eyes.

The Buckeyes had an excellent team that year. Quarterback Mike Tomczak and receiver Cris Carter were two of the best players in the nation. Ohio State's blockers were big, fast, and powerful. The team's defense was led by Pepper Johnson and Chris Spielman, who would later become NFL stars.

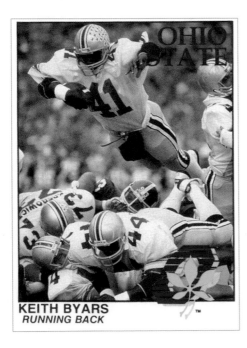

KEITH BYARS
RUNNING BACK

This day, however, belonged to Keith Byars. After Illinois opened a 24–0 lead in the second quarter, the Buckeyes looked to their big running back to help save the day. Byars smashed into the Illinois line again and again. He gained 274 yards and scored five touchdowns—including the game-winner with less than a minute left.

The most amazing play of the day came in the third quarter. With Illinois

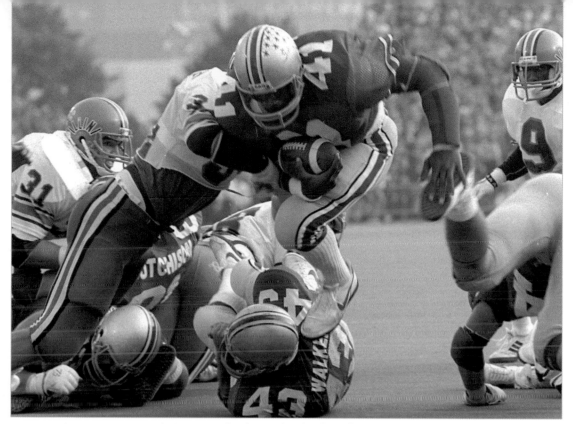

expecting a pass, Tomczak handed the ball to Byars, who broke through the line and swerved toward the right sideline. He was running at full speed when he saw a group of tacklers trying to cut him off. In a flash, Byars darted to his left and ran the rest of the way for a 67-yard touchdown.

As Byars crossed the goal line, the fans realized that he was wearing only one shoe. His other shoe was back on the right sideline, where he had made his great move. Teammate Jim Lachey picked up the shoe and was amazed to see that the laces were still tied tightly. Byars was not sure how it happened, but he literally ran out of his shoe!

LEFT: A trading card featuring Keith Byars.
ABOVE: Byars powers through the Illinois defense.

Team Spirit

Ohio State's greatest football tradition is the marching band's halftime formation, which spells out *O-h-i-o* in script letters. It takes hundreds of hours of practice, and there is no room for mistakes. One of the school's greatest honors is the chance to dot the *i*. The band has two fight songs—"The Buckeye Battle Cry" and "Across the Field"—but it also plays a hit song from the 1960s, "Hang on Sloopy."

Many students who attend Ohio State games form a large cheering section called the "Block O." They sit near the end zone in the open part of Ohio Stadium. The fans there start many cheers (including "O-H-I-O") that work their way around the entire stadium. They often get help from Brutus Buckeye, a **mascot** with a head shaped like a nut. He has been a part of Ohio State games since the 1960s. When the Buckeyes win, the Victory Bell sounds to share the good news with everyone on campus.

LEFT: Brutus Buckeye leads Ohio State onto the field.
ABOVE: A pin showing Buckeyes team spirit.

Timeline

At the end of each college season, the best teams are invited to play in special "Bowl" games, such as the Rose Bowl, **Orange Bowl**, and **Sugar Bowl**. Bowl games usually take place in January, but they count in the final rankings of the previous season. That means the top team in 2007 wasn't decided until early 2008. In this timeline, bowl games are listed in the year they were held.

1919
Ohio State beats Michigan for the first time.

1950
The team wins its first Rose Bowl.

1890
The Buckeyes play their first game, against Ohio Wesleyan.

1930
Wes Fesler is named Big Ten MVP.

1936
The Ohio State marching band performs "script Ohio" for the first time.

Wes Fesler

The famous "script Ohio."

Art Schlichter drops back to pass.

1975
Archie Griffin wins his second Heisman Trophy.

1981
Art Schlichter sets a team record with 7,547 career passing yards.

2002
Ohio State wins the national championship.

1969
The Buckeyes win the Rose Bowl and claim their fifth national championship.

1978
Woody Hayes wins his 200th game at Ohio State.

1997
The Buckeyes win their sixth Rose Bowl.

A 1969 Rose Bowl pennant.

This pin celebrates Ohio State's 2002 championship.

Fun Facts

LISTEN TO THE MUSIC

Since 1932, the Ohio State marching band has held a rehearsal known as the "Skull Session" before every home game. It became so popular that the band moved to the St. John Arena on campus to allow more fans to attend.

DANCING KING

One of Ohio State's most famous fans was Orlas King. During timeouts at home games, he would dance to a song called "Neutron Dance." King passed away in 2004. The Buckeyes and their fans honored him with a moment of silence, and the band then played King's song.

DYNAMIC DUO

Although Archie Griffin is Ohio State's most famous runner, his teammate Pete Johnson holds the school records for touchdowns in a season (26) and a career (56).

RUBBING IT IN

In 1968, the Buckeyes scored a fourth-quarter touchdown against arch-rival Michigan to make the score 50–14. Woody Hayes ordered his players to go for two points instead of one, even though the Buckeyes had the game won. When asked why he went for two, Hayes said, "Because I couldn't go for three!"

GO FOR THE GOLD

Whenever Ohio State beats Michigan, the coaches and players receive a gold charm that looks like a pair of football pants. The tradition started in 1934 after Buckeyes coach Francis Schmidt challenged his team to defeat the Wolverines. "They put their pants on one leg at a time just like everyone else," Schmidt reminded his players.

SENSATIONAL SEVEN

As of 2007, seven Buckeyes players and coaches had been voted into the **Pro Football Hall of Fame**—Sid Gillman, Lou Groza, Dante Lavelli, Jim Parker, Paul Warfield, Bill Willis, and Paul Brown.

LEFT: Pete Johnson   **ABOVE**: Lou Groza

For the Record

T he great Buckeyes teams and players have left their marks on the record books. These are the "best of the best" …

BUCKEYES AWARD WINNERS

HEISMAN TROPHY
TOP COLLEGE PLAYER

Les Horvath	1944
Vic Janowicz	1950
Hopalong Cassady	1955
Archie Griffin	1974
Archie Griffin	1975
Eddie George	1995
Troy Smith	2006

MAXWELL AWARD
TOP COLLEGE PLAYER

Hopalong Cassady	1955
Bob Ferguson	1961
Archie Griffin	1975
Eddie George	1995

WALTER CAMP AWARD
TOP COLLEGE PLAYER

Archie Griffin	1974
Archie Griffin	1975
Eddie George	1995
Troy Smith	2006

RIMINGTON AWARD
TOP CENTER

LeCharles Bentley	2001

DAVEY O'BRIEN AWARD
TOP QUARTERBACK

Troy Smith	2006

DOAK WALKER AWARD
TOP RUNNING BACK

Eddie George	1995

FRED BILETNIKOFF AWARD
TOP RECEIVER

Terry Glenn	1995

LOU GROZA AWARD
TOP PLACE-KICKER

Mike Nugent	2004

RAY GUY AWARD
TOP PUNTER

B.J. Sander	2003

JIM THORPE AWARD
TOP DEFENSIVE BACK

Antoine Winfield	1998

OUTLAND TROPHY
TOP LINEMAN

Jim Parker	1956
Jim Stillwagon	1970
John Hicks	1973
Orlando Pace	1996

VINCE LOMBARDI AWARD
TOP LINEMAN

Jim Stillwagon	1970
John Hicks	1973
Chris Spielman	1987
Orlando Pace	1995
Orlando Pace	1996
A.J. Hawk	2005

BRONKO NAGURSKI AWARD
TOP DEFENSIVE PLAYER

James Laurinaitis	2006

DICK BUTKUS AWARD
TOP LINEBACKER

Andy Katzenmoyer	1997
James Laurinaitis	2007

OHIO STATE

JIM STILLWAGON
MIDDLE GUARD

Jim Stillwagon

A.J. HAWK

A.J. Hawk

The Buckeyes went to the 1958 Rose Bowl after winning the 1957 Big Ten title.

Rose Bowl Classic   OHIO STATE 1958   Buckeyes

BUCKEYES ACHIEVEMENTS

ACHIEVEMENT	YEAR
Conference Champions	1916
Conference Champions	1917
Conference Champions	1920
Conference Champions	1935
Conference Champions	1939
Conference Champions	1942
National Champions	1942
Conference Champions	1944
Conference Champions	1949
Conference Champions	1954
National Champions	1954
Conference Champions	1955
Conference Champions	1957
National Champions	1957
Conference Champions	1961
National Champions	1961
Conference Champions	1968
National Champions	1968
Conference Champions	1969
Conference Champions	1970
National Champions	1970
Conference Champions	1972
Conference Champions	1973
Conference Champions	1974
Conference Champions	1975
Conference Champions	1976
Conference Champions	1977
Conference Champions	1979
Conference Champions	1981
Conference Champions	1984
Conference Champions	1986
Conference Champions	1993
Conference Champions	1996
Conference Champions	1998
Conference Champions	2002
National Champions	2002
Conference Champions	2005
Conference Champions	2006
Conference Champions	2007

OHIO STATE

JAMES PARKER
GUARD

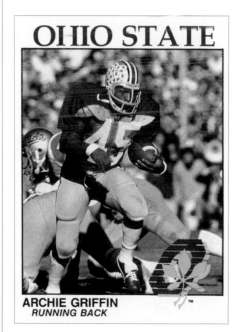

OHIO STATE

ARCHIE GRIFFIN
RUNNING BACK

TOP: Jim Parker
ABOVE: Archie Griffin

The Big Ten

Ohio State is a member of the Big Ten Conference, the oldest college sports conference in America. Over the years, the Big Ten actually expanded to 11 teams. These are the Buckeyes' neighbors …

THE BIG TEN

1 University of Illinois Fighting Illini
Urbana-Champaign, Illinois

2 Indiana University Hoosiers
Bloomington, Indiana

3 University of Iowa Hawkeyes
Iowa City, Iowa

4 University of Michigan Wolverines
Ann Arbor, Michigan

5 Michigan State University Spartans
East Lansing, Michigan

6 University of Minnesota Golden Gophers
Minneapolis and Saint Paul, Minnesota

7 Northwestern University Wildcats
Evanston, Illinois

8 Ohio State University Buckeyes
Columbus, Ohio

9 Pennsylvania State University Nittany Lions*
University Park, Pennsylvania

10 Purdue University Boilermakers
West Lafayette, Indiana

11 University of Wisconsin Badgers
Madison, Wisconsin

* Penn State joined the Big Ten in 1993.

The College Game

College football may look like the same game you see NFL teams play on Sundays, but there are some important differences. The first is that most college games take place on Saturday. This has been true for more than 100 years. Below are several other differences between college and pro football.

CLASS NOTES

College players are younger than NFL players. They are student-athletes who have graduated from high school and now play on their college's varsity team, which is the highest level of competition. Most are between the ages of 18 and 22.

College players are allowed to compete for four seasons. Each year is given a different name or "class"—freshman (first year), sophomore (second year), junior (third year), and senior (fourth year). Players who are unable to play for the varsity can remain in the same class for an extra year. This is called "red-shirting." These players are still students and must attend classes during their extra year.

RULE BOOK

There are several differences between the rules in college football and the NFL. Here are the important ones: 1) In college, a play ends as soon as the ball carrier's knee touches the ground, even if he slips or dives. In the NFL, a player must be tackled. 2) In college, a player catching the ball near the sideline must have one foot in bounds for the reception to count. In the NFL, a player must have both feet in bounds. 3) Since 1996, tie games in college have been decided by a special overtime period. Each team is given a chance to score from its opponent's 25-yard line. In the NFL, the first team to score in overtime is the winner.

WHO'S NUMBER 1?

How is the national champion of college football decided? Each week during the season, teams are ranked from best to worst in several different polls of coaches and sportswriters. These rankings are based on many factors, including a team's record and the level of competition that it has played. At the end of the year, the two top-ranked teams play each other. The winner is declared the national champion. This tradition started in 1998 when college football began using the **Bowl Championship Series (BCS)**. Prior to that year, the top two teams did not always face each other. Sometimes, that made it very difficult to decide which school was the best.

CONFERENCE CALL

Most colleges are members of athletic conferences. Each conference represents a different part of the country. For example, the Atlantic Coast Conference is made up of teams from up and down the East Coast. Teams that belong to a conference are required to play a certain number of games against the other teams in their conference. At the end of the year, the team with the best record is crowned conference champion (unless the league holds a championship game). Teams also play schools from outside their conference. Wins and losses in those games do not count in the conference standings. However, they are very important to a team's national ranking.

BOWL GAMES

Bowl games—such as the Rose Bowl, Sugar Bowl, and Orange Bowl—are extra games played at the end of each season. Bowl games give fans a chance to see the best teams from around the country play one another. These games are scheduled during the Christmas and New Year's holiday season, so students are free to travel to the cities where bowl games are played. There are now more than 25 bowl games.

Since 1998, the BCS has selected the nation's very best teams and carefully matched them in a handful of bowl games. The BCS chooses the champions of major conferences, as well as other schools with talented teams. The two top-ranked teams meet in the BCS title game for the national championship.

Glossary

ALL-AMERICANS—College players voted as the best at their positions.

BIG TEN CONFERENCE—A league for colleges located in Illinois, Indiana, Iowa, Michigan, Minnesota, Ohio, Pennsylvania, and Wisconsin.

BLOCKER—A player who protects the ball carrier with his body.

BOWL CHAMPIONSHIP SERIES (BCS)—The system used by college football to select the best two teams to play for the national championship each season. Before the BCS came along, the national championship was unofficial, and more than one team often claimed they were the best.

FIESTA BOWL—The annual bowl game played in Glendale, Arizona. The first Fiesta Bowl was played in 1971.

FUMBLED—Dropped the ball while carrying it.

GOAL-LINE STAND—Attempt by the defense to stop an opponent that is very close to the goal line.

HEISMAN TROPHY—The award given each year to the best player in college football.

INTERCEPTED—Caught in the air by a defensive player.

LINEUP—The list of players in a game.

MOST VALUABLE PLAYER (MVP)—The award given to the best player in each bowl game.

NATIONAL FOOTBALL LEAGUE (NFL)—The league that started in 1920 and is still operating today.

ORANGE BOWL—The annual bowl game played in Miami, Florida. The first Orange Bowl was played in 1935.

OVERTIME—The extra period played when a game is tied after 60 minutes.

PRO FOOTBALL HALL OF FAME—The museum in Canton, Ohio, where football's greatest players are honored. A player voted into the Hall of Fame is sometimes called a "Hall of Famer."

PROFESSIONAL—A player or team that plays a sport for money. College players are not paid, so they are considered "amateurs."

ROSE BOWL—The annual bowl game played in Pasadena, California. The Tournament of Roses Parade takes place before the game. The first Rose Bowl was played in 1902.

ROSTER—The list of a team's active players.

SUGAR BOWL—The annual bowl game played in New Orleans, Louisiana. The first Sugar Bowl was played in 1935.

TAILBACK—A position created when football first started. Depending on the play, a tailback would run or throw, or try to catch a pass.

OTHER WORDS TO KNOW

ARTIFICIAL—Made by people, not nature.

CAMPUS—The grounds and buildings of a college.

CENTURY—A period of 100 years.

DECADES—Periods of 10 years; also specific periods, such as the 1950s.

ENLISTED—Signed up for.

ENTHUSIASTIC—Filled with strong excitement.

MASCOT—An animal or person believed to bring a group good luck.

OLD-TIMERS—People who have been alive for a long time.

OUTSMART—Get the better of by being clever.

ROUT—A lopsided victory.

SENSATIONAL—Amazing.

TAILBONE—The bone that protects the base of the spine.

TRADITION—A belief or custom that is handed down from generation to generation.

UNDEFEATED—Without a loss.

Places to Go

ON THE ROAD

OHIO STATE UNIVERSITY
410 Woody Hayes Drive
Columbus, Ohio 43210
(614) 292-7572

COLLEGE FOOTBALL HALL OF FAME
111 South St. Joseph Street
South Bend, Indiana 46601
(800) 440-3263

ON THE WEB

THE OHIO STATE BUCKEYES   www.ohiostatebuckeyes.com
  • *Learn more about the Buckeyes*

BIG TEN CONFERENCE   bigten.cstv.com
  • *Learn more about the Big Ten teams*

COLLEGE FOOTBALL HALL OF FAME   www.collegefootball.org
  • *Learn more about college football*

ON THE BOOKSHELF

To learn more about the sport of football, look for these books at your library or bookstore:

  • Kaufman, Gabriel. *Football in the Big Ten*. New York, New York: Rosen Central, 2008.
  • DeCock, Luke. *Great Teams in College Football History*. Chicago, Illinois: Raintree, 2006.
  • Yuen, Kevin. *The 10 Most Intense College Football Rivalries*. New York, New York: Franklin Watts, 2008.

Index

PAGE NUMBERS IN **BOLD** REFER TO ILLUSTRATIONS.

About the Author

MARK STEWART has written more than 30 books on football players and teams, and over 100 sports books for kids. He has also interviewed dozens of athletes, politicians, and celebrities. Although Mark grew up in New York City, as a young fan he loved Big Ten football. He remembers the amazing Buckeyes of 1968 and the great running of Archie Griffin in the 1970s. Mark comes from a family of writers. His grandfather was Sunday Editor of *The New York Time*s and his mother was Articles Editor for *Ladies' Home Journal* and *McCall's*. Mark became interested in sports during lazy summer days spent at the Connecticut home of his father's godfather, sportswriter John R. Tunis. Mark is a graduate of Duke University, with a degree in History. He lives with his wife Sarah, and daughters Mariah and Rachel, overlooking Sandy Hook, New Jersey.